STILL THIS NEED

Still This Need

First edition © The Heaventree Press 2009
All work © Michael McKimm 2009
All rights reserved
ISBN 978-1-906038-30-4

Cover art: 'Rock Pools in Water / Worn Recrystallised Limestone'
© Ted Nield 2009
Heaventree logo design by Panna Chauhan

Published in the UK by
The Heaventree Press,
Institute for Creative Enterprise,
Puma Way, Coventry Technology Park
CV1 2TT

Printed in the UK by
Cromwell Press Group, Trowbridge, Wiltshire

We are grateful for the financial support of

STILL THIS NEED

Michael McKimm

The Heaventree Press

ACKNOWLEDGEMENTS

Acknowledgements are due to the editors of the following publications where some of these poems, or versions of them, first appeared: *Gists and Piths, Heaventree New Poets Volume 1* (Heaventree, 2004), *Horizon Review, The Interpreter's House, Magma, Oxford Poetry, Phoenix New Writing* (Heaventree, 2004), *PN Review, Sherb: New Urban Writing from Coventry* (Heaventree, 2006), *The Shuffle Anthology* (The Shuffle Press, 2008), *The Warwick Review* and *The Wolf*. A version of 'Resurrection' was published by *Dossier Journal* (New York) in collaboration with Alastair McKimm.

'The Granite State' and 'Victoria Park, December' were originally commissioned by Roddy Lumsden for multi-poet readings in London.

Thanks, for their advice and support with this collection, to Luigi Coppola, Michael Hulse, Roddy Lumsden, David Morley, Jonathan Morley and especially Zachary Lamdin.

FOR MY PARENTS
BROTHER AND SISTERS
AND IN MEMORY OF
ROBERT 'BERT' MCKIMM
1912 - 2003

CONTENTS

Fledgling

This is the time of night
when freight trains start to rumble past
  and flicker their electric lights
  and let off their sharp blasts.
I'd just got off to sleep at last,

  it seems, but now awake
I want to conjure up a bird,
  for you, a lapwing, a corncrake,
  a teal – those ones you've heard
me list before. Without a word

  I'll bring it to the bed,
this quiet living thing, this gift
  of air, and set it by your head,
  and add my own and drift
towards slumber. For what else could lift

  me off to sleep except
a grounded bird to keep an eye
  on our slight bodies – unslept –
  exhausted by surprise,
  two timid fledglings in the sky?

The Rookery

for Anthony Taylor, who was burned out, 2005

He showed me where the rooks had made their nests
amongst the chestnut trees behind his house.
Weightier noise had not been heard before,
the high-pitched lumber of their working calls,
to build those nests, to build that fort of nests.
And the missiles that we dodged, air defence,
sticks and nuts, chunks of bark and shit, and noise,
noise their best defence. We hid there in
the shelter of the sheugh and let them hush
their panicked calls, and let them rest their beaks,
their breaths, and let the coastline quieten,
until, who knows what set it off – a branch
snapped somewhere in the woods, a fallen cone –
the black wave buckled into flight, an arch
of noise and weight and always looping back.

Cartographers on Errigal

Nimh: Poison (Gaelic) *Neamh*: Heaven (Gaelic)

Scatch-grass and slow water, wild-roaming lambs.
This is what we take in on the walk
through briars and whins, until we start to climb
the hulk of rock, moon rock, unfathomable rock,
patched in the crimson blood of Balor slain
by Lugh, and the quartzite white that cakes
its peak and shines a beacon on the glen,
and sends the light in bolts across the lake.

The English, when they came here, named it 'Poison'
and that is how it stands. The two words were
the same to them, their vowels different,
and too few listened when the troops were sent
to take the stock of a shattered farmer:
'Heaven, this is the place we call heaven.'

Aran

He schooled in Irish on the island
and culled his crop from simple life.

Each morning brought
a fog of gulls,
the tender sound
of boys' feet crunching kelp.

He later faced the shot-filled barrel
which brought to mind the anus of a ewe,
snug against his face
as he helped it lamb.

Martello

March 2003

> For Joyce
> the tower was home.
> > Isolated, quiet,
> > beyond the touch of days and hours,
> > > so still.

> But this
> Martello tower
> > was built for war, no more
> > than shelter from Napoleon
> > > the Great.

> What fear
> could drive those men
> > to build them all over
> > the colonies? South Africa,
> > > Ceylon,

> then north
> America,
> and here, Magilligan,
> this lonely sharp jut of County
> > > Derry,

> where I
> stand still and face
> > the shore, that other land,
> > and listen to news of each threat,
> > > each choice.

The Burial

Despite the fear, the knowing lurch of what he'd lost
and could in future lose, there was still the need.

He headed east in spring, Dunseverick, Ballintoy,
under the red bulk of Knocklayd, where the road

swerved through banks of mottled gorse, and the rock,
carved out like a piece of wood that's lathed and turned,

produced the forest park where it had happened
fifteen years before: the unforgivable, taken

as a given. He bought an ice cream from the vendor
and asked himself, *Am I remembered here? Or has*

it been too long? He had stood there a thousand times,
it seemed, always when the light was high on the lip

of the glen, and the cold sent a shudder to the spine
and the wind would find its silence. For there was still

the need, to stand beneath the trees and smell the soil,
the furring bark, and watch the hedge-line redden

in the dusk. He closed his eyes and listened to the rustle
of the leaves up in the dark, and shivered as it all

came back to him: the unremarkable hatchbacks,
the pick-axe and the shovels, the way the earth turned

easily under the weight of his foot, the edge of the spade.
Then the smouldering unrest of the life he'd made.

Resurrection

As the cod that's cooked in a mountain
of salt comes out delicate as butter, a fur
of disappearances, unrecognisable,
so have I buried the book of our lives
in the salt mines of Cheshire, twenty
miles of white tunnels, two hundred feet deep.
I have taken a knife and carved out a shelf
and placed there the first time we met,
the bar where I read you my poems,
the movies we watched, the first piece of furniture
you bolted together, the meals that we ate;
I have stored them in salt where they will
be dry, not feel the touch of blight:
these thoughts, these kisses, these places,
this memory of a white fish becoming tongue,
mouth, throat, disappearing into your body

Still Life

All Hallow's Eve, another vixen fresh off Hackney Marsh,
her voice loud, screeching, sensing rivals, enemies,
the loose bins out back. You have your head low
under the white blinds, watching her frozen
by the parked cars, a keen eye on the shadows.
She is healthy, plumped up, with a good coat.
Each night this week we've had the foxes bait us
from our dreams; they patrol the crisscrossed streets
and duck through hedges on the parks of the estates.
We saw three, mother and two cubs, peering at us
from a garage roof, nonplussed, inquisitive.

We try so much to live our lives beyond our lives
and what we see in front of us: new year, blue sky,
frost on the footpath, people dumbed by summer,
blowing at fists; the nights drawing in and the cold snap
descending like a benediction; the foxes sharing our streets,
the way they have always seen you before you see them.

Victoria Park, December

He heard while he sang and dreamed
A piper piping away,
And never was piping so sad,
And never was piping so gay.

— W. B. Yeats, 'The Host of the Air'

We were still in the park when the music started –
choral, first seasonal hymns in the half-dark
of the bandstand, the pent-up warm-ups of brass
and pipes, four men neatly starched and collared,
a circle of singers. You went towards them enamoured,
and we stood two duffelled-lovers-dreaming
in the steady wind-fixed music, daydreaming,
each band of notes and chords a string in the stomach
pulling us like children pulled from Hamelin.
I dreamed of the day and the day's slow happenings.
That morning my mother had called with news
about her ribs, the unseen bruising colouring inside her.
How is she so old, I asked myself, my voice
out loud, woken. You held me then,
and we forgot about the cold, how cold it gets,
each winter's liturgy of frost-bit staupings
in the mud; brittle reeds, the bearded-heron
shivering by the lake; and the pipes erupting in our street,
Victorian leaden things suddenly frozen, broken.

The Lammas Lands

Six Poems for Hackney Marsh

What I shall miss is the smell at the end
of the street, the sound of water gushing
under Hackney – marsh-water, Lea Valley
tribulations, all that's dank and dead
in hidden liquid: history mainly, flooded
plains scuttling Viking warships, sewer-tales
and monies made from bodies, layers of clay
and chalk and once crisp water, drinkable
by seamen down at Limehouse. If you think
of water as the thing that builds a town
you can't imagine living where the river
doesn't run, even if that river is a stream
that swells with rainfall, coming up from drains
and forever whispering beneath your feet.

This is where King Alfred beached the Danes,
cut channels in the Lea, created the marsh
and, post battle, post hot-scorched summer,
post heady festival of *loafmass*, gave it over
kindly to the serfs as common land, to graze
their cattle, tackle the unshod horses.
Land too thick for crops, too wet for housing,
land wept cunningly from warfare, strategy,
pre-planned hard labour of soldiers and slaves,
was meted out – piecemeal – between
August and March, as feeding space, lambing
land, recreation ground, where people came
from the parishes of Homerton and Hackney
to break the bread, to celebrate the harvest.

There is a white wind and a clanging bell
across the marsh, a frisson in the wires
that slice the pitches, where ping on leather
meets the thump of white-paint post, branches
clacking in the trees, tarpaulin unravelling
on the building sites: grit, sand and aggregate.
Think of the causeway that the Romans built
to keep their road going straight to Colchester,
a heap of shale and shattered boulders paved
with smoother slabs set into concrete, the coarse
rudus, the soft *nucleus*, then curved to let
rainwater slip into the fields. Suddenly
there is an army cutting a line through
the Sunday fixtures, a legion of pall bearers.

Cormorants are landing on the Lammas Lands.
We watch them from the side of the canal,
four black phantoms coming in slow from the north,
all hush-hush, wings arched for the descent,
feet carving a line, long bodies glistening
in the water. Someone needs to document
the birds that use these reaches for their nests:
herons, grebes and ruddy ducks, great groups
of Canada geese, reed buntings calling thinly
from the willow, the pecking war of coots
and moorhens, the fearful jays, the timid teal,
but mostly the stealth-breaking cormorants,
drying their wings on the branches of trees,
like standards on the blue shield of the sky.

In creating the Marsh they created
an island. Surprisingly sensible
a solution: appease the bargemen
and the mill owners, let the New River
Company have their fill for Londoners.
Simply cut a canal and let the water
take a different course twice over,
one for cargoes up and down from Hertford,
one to turn the stones and grind the corn
to flour. That was that, flat unbuilt land
lurching southwards towards the Isle of Dogs;
whitewashed lock-side pubs, fishermen
relishing the pike; a reservoir, reserve,
an archipelago conjured by commerce.

Soon the allotments will be deserted.
Ray from Bow has made his special salad,
the Cypriot Hassim has sliced his spuds,
nurtured them with salt. In the work shed
they've laid out the last of the harvest,
grapes and olives, leeks, cabbages, parsnips.
Along with the carrots and beets, from
the damp earth they've pulled up their thoughts:
dreams of better lives, the thrill of putting down
a deposit, inheritance; the idea that a square
patch of London could breed dates, callaloo,
sweet potatoes the size of your head,
things not seen since childhood, homeland,
the family hearth, some long forgotten feast.

The Underground

When the lights went out in the station
and the shrill of panic rose as some people
stopped and others kept on walking,
I thought of mining and the heat of mines,
the cage going down with the men packed
and joking, the taste of the first cigarette
still tart on their lips, then the smell
of the coal or salt or sulphur, especially the sulphur –
the great stenches of the innards of the earth.
The way the skin, litmus-like, imbibes
the dust and grit, the mass of molecules
in the air; the way our throats are closing
now the more we breathe; and how all week
there's been this talk of switching off the lights –
I thought of this as the fear entered my groin
like butterflies who find themselves too far south
in spring, their wings singed and browning at the edges.

Coventry

Look at the map. This is where the river meets
the pavement, slips in secret beneath the ground.

Our feet tread on concrete, brick and earth
and echo over water. I cannot decide which way

it travels through this city; I am no diviner.
We look for patterns in side streets and avenues.

Does it really keep on going or does it simply end
with the cut on the paper? All is guesswork.

Now you see the city for what it is, an infiltration
on a lake brimming with laughing geese,

a river that shallowed for the wheels of passing carts
now a tunnel, a trickle through coal-seams,

water passing through the crypts, the un-dug catacombs,
seeping into the foundations and cracking the marble.

Imagine you could navigate this city on a boat,
misspent beside the trundle of traffic. You laugh now.

But look at the map. Imagine an orchard of streetnames
watered by centuries: *Gosford, Bailey, The Burges, Spon.*

Blue

What I should like to find out is the effect of an intenser blue in the sky
— Vincent Van Gogh

I

Midnight, and moonlight feathering the sea
between Punta Galera and Sa Conillera,

and beyond that too, so where the lighthouse
pinpricks the darkness is like the prow

of a great ship anchored down but rocking,
its crew and captain slumbering towards daybreak.

Landmass is what complements the water,
not the other way around. The blueness

is the ink invading crevices in paper,
that says if needed it could accomplish all.

At night it is still blue, almost navy
where it creeps into the cove, a fabric woven

with salt, plankton, seaflints, beneath
a startling sky, needled by Venus.

II

Do we adapt to the noise of a lawnmower
the way we get used to the rasp of *cicadas,*

these daybugs existing in phonics, powerful, unseen?
Maybe they keep us sane in the stillness, where

nothing moves in the air, too hot for birds,
and the wind is a tepid thing. Between

myself and the horizon there are fifteen shades

of blue: the lagoon of the swimming-pool,

dark blobs on terracotta lanterns, a hue on branches,
humped mountains, cobalt rivets in burnt rocks,

afterflow and stretchmarks on the sea,
turning in like furrows in a field.

The sky itself is first invented blue, assured
and unsurpassed, the blue of void and distance.

III

On the streets of Eivissa we hypothesise
lamplit fingers, St. Cyriac guiding the Catalans

through the walls of the city, battlements
so thick that tunnels run inside them

and all that's known is what is felt
in darkness: cobbles and earth-dry bricks,

a broken stone, the curve of a pathway,
the echo of footsteps, and what's recorded

only by its absence – the colour of clothing,
the shape of a smile. Funny how we think

thought craves the darkness, when really
the migraine of light is what we always head for,

fresh air, the wide birthright of sky,
all that's wanted and perpetual and elusive.

Squam Lake

She dropped the playing cards and made a brisk 'Shush!'
A moth battled with the mesh over the window,
the little electric light emitted a low buzz.
That was all. I told her that *she* was a loon

and slinked off to my small motel room,
perched over the lake, lit by fireflies.
But lying there, all I could think about
was listening, hearing a great ululation
coming off the black water.
                            Then I heard her,
tiptoeing across the kitchen, opening the latch
and slipping onto the netted balcony.

The Spot

They've come to count the birds this winter morning,
stand twitchy in the kitchen as the light
comes slowly from the darkness, blue and low,
and the farmers return from the day's first milk.
What unlikely prospectors of faith,
eight men and two women, thick wrapped
and high-booted, hair like downy leaf
under woollen caps, sipping tea and thinking
of what they might have failed to think about:
sea fog predicted for the afternoon,
Ordnance maps in cling film, squares of chamois,
the filaments in old flasks holding out;
of stonechats and linnets, shrikes and dunnocks,
of days spent high in barns and seeing nought,
the cleck of hens, the fox's bloody mouth.
They're quiet of the need to see again
their favourite spots: a corncrake in the reeds,
lapwings dancing, cranes breeding on the broads,
and, for the old man, rubbing grit off a lens,
a great beaked red parrot, up in the tree
as he swigged his canteen. They leave their mugs
and thank the farmer's wife. She walks to the gate
and watches as they totter towards the fields,
eight men and two women, notebooks in hands,
backs arched forward in the January winds.

The Old Coach-House, Cark

for Flora Ellison

As light comes into a temple, sun's orb
cut at right angles, a shaft widening
on the marble, the morning opens up here
as bright light on old stonework,
cobwebs caught in rafters, shine in woodgrain,
an earthly stillness, something long forgotten.
We seemed to drive all night into the dark,
skins of lorries flapping in the headlights,
then fell to dreams of cows' tongues at the glass,
a jigsaw left scattered, whitened antlers,
Queen Victoria frowning in the bathroom.
Now the morning is a house packed with books,
the smell of bacon spitting on the pan,
my hand going out to touch the cold stone,
fingers mapping dry trails in the grout.
You might have thought the thrill would be
the birds we'd seen on the road to Windermere,
this day of scenic routes: ducks and swans,
pheasants, jackdaws, peregrines. But instead
I want to write about the heat that's found in stonework,
the pulse of years of permanence and change,
voices broken over time, the phantoms found here.
Your heart, your sanctuary; this ancestral house.

The Cycling Geologist

Grenville Arthur James Cole (1859-1924)

Excursion 1: The Gypsy Road

Poland first, and the minerals of Myslenice,
then across the alluvial plains, and up through
the Tatra mountains, Grenville on the three-wheeled
Humber-Beeston, Gerald Butler in the crow's nest,
the old penny-farthing, keeping a fair speed, cutting
through limestone, a curious couple, unused to the heat,
unused to the local uses of language, when to speak German
and when to speak English, and when either would see a slammed door.
With the help of strong thighs they entered the Alps,
cooled tired muscles in the river at Garam,
stopped off to see the mines at Hajnik, at Schopferstollen
ran fingers across the silver, two Slovakian boys
holding the lanterns, beaming at payment, then
the cone at Schladinberg, and the burning coals
near Dux (*Oligocene, Miocene*), burning, still
and always burning – how he found the time to note
the sediments, scribble down his verses on volcanoes,
collect and store the fragments for his students –
one thousand and fifty miles in thirty-eight days,
Krakow to Coblentz, the legs turning, the tinkle
of stones in the spokes, the odd whirr of wheels
startling horses. You can never imagine a grimace,
a face strained at a hill, but it must have been there.
Instead there is only the thought of him smiling,
free-wheeling past olive groves, leaning back his sun-hatted head
and shouting to Butler in the gods: 'It is wonderful
what amount of rock has to be cut away before
you can make a decently artistic mountain.'

Excursion 2: As We Ride

It had been her idea to cycle down the aisle,
and Grenville, still so much her tutor, had agreed;
it was like they'd cycled from the church and never stopped,
honeymoon turned lifelong expedition, France, Germany,
Poland and the Balkans, and Ireland too, her homeland
and his home. What he made of rocks she made of people:
cold and brittle, overwhelming, or, uniquely interesting,
made with the sort of edge that will take three years
to understand, such time to stop not known on their itinerary.
Sometimes they grew tired.
There is a photograph of her, circa 1900, sheltering
beneath a tree, her head resting in her hands, fed up,
watching her husband pull off his boot, their bikes
stacked on the verge. But she fell in love with Orahova,
and so did he, the small town deep between iced mountains,
the name they chose for their home in Carrickmines.

Excursion 3: Ireland Student Trip 1903

Dalradian, Silurian, Carboniferous.
It was an unknown language for the west,
a queer way to talk of Mayo, the gristly bogs
of Galway. The boys made notes studiously,
and one stopped to snap the teacher's 'Roadster'
beneath Croagh Patrick, or maybe he snapped it
himself, the tool of the new evangelism, funded
by the State, peddling talk of millions
east through Omagh, under Slieve Gallion
to the Antrim Plateau – *gneissic, Tertiary, Cretaceous.*
They rooted around in Kilroot for salts from the Triassic,
then belted down to Belfast to chip off basalt
from Cave Hill, and on the last day, up at the crack
of dawn, they scaled Slieve Donard, watched the light
moving barren and brown across the Mournes.
Oh for a last free-wheel, he thought, his legs
beginning to seize, his hands locked tight
on the bars, (the funding stopped).
Oh for another hundred million years of cycling!
   A zip down
mountains with the wind moaning softly in the pass.

Cemetery

Why do midges linger here to choke us?
Too easily presumed the resurrected,
they are clumps of motion, thickets shifting
in the thundery air. They don't give a damn

for yew trees, the poisonous necessity
that colonnades the leaf-bark path,
in this, the only sculpture park in town,
deserted but for dogs and lonely men.

Architecture crumbles in neglect, where
we feign an interest in unknown chiselled names
and try to tell which dead have not resurfaced
in a footnote, have been unlucky

with the bodysnatchers – no glib remark,
no coins left falling from their mouths.
Lately we have found ourselves a niche
in worrying away at others' legacies,

not haunted by what lies in dormant pits,
inscriptions on gravestones, the actual bones,
the cavalcade of mourners on the London Road,
the chapels, mausoleums, the corner for the Jews,

but by what still soars beyond the boundaries,
memories as rested as these children
born in limbo. Here's the suggestion:
pull down a yew branch, fashion the long-bow.

Children of Lir

They went on then west to Loch Dairbhreach, the Lake of the Oaks, and the horses were stopped there, and Aoife bade the children of Lir to go out and bathe in the lake, and they did as she bade them. And as soon as Aoife saw them out in the lake she struck them with a Druid rod, and put on them the shape of four swans, white and beautiful.
— translated from the Irish by Lady Gregory

Inside the swan we pedalled mightily.
This was a rare treat. A wee jaunt
to Bangor for the day, and a ride
across the lake on wings of fibreglass.

It was the last day of summer
and I was resolute in my demands.
'I amn't goin' to school tomorrow'
was all I knew and stuck by,

pedalling away all by myself,
turning and turning in the shallow water,
chanting 'amn't amn't amn't'
like a spell that would not work for trying.

And then everything takes flight.
I'm lifting off in another artificial bird
and coming down in the rainy light of Belfast,
busy talking about life across the water,

when you laugh and say I've learnt to speak
like them, that I'd found the g in going,
substituted all my eager slang,
let every accent infiltrate my speech.

But there was something else. I caught you staring
from the bottom of the stairs
with a look that said no more than
'I don't understand how much you've changed.'

Yet once a week or so, you must know
that you're the one that brings me back with words,
your incantations down the phone lines:
hoke, boke, wee, wick, dram, bog, aye.

Out of the swan, I cry, pull a face,
while you smile and cast another spell
which makes me shiver:
If the wind changes you'll be like that forever.

The History Lesson

I thought I was so clever with that pun –
'An Aud Affair' – that those three words somehow lent
a hand to history, laid to rest the sodden, sinking guns.
You matched me with 'A Tale of Two Casements',
as smug a headline as the *Irish Times*
could ever print of Roger and his German sub,
surfacing as the red hand of his crimes.

*

It was just a matter
of means when
my fives times great

grandfather boarded a ship
from Scotland in 1775
and became (by the accident

of labels) an Ulster Scot,
leading through happenstance
and little tweaking chances

of birth and survival
to me, twelve years old,
got up in Union stripes

with a new backpack
and dinner money:
red, white and blue

from my neck
to my waist. Simply
no choice, I mean.

*

We wrote epitaphs in biro,
summing up key points
with clumsy rhymes:

Wolfe Tone *all alone*.
Curragh Mutiny *under scrutiny*.
Easter Rising, *unsurprising*.
Black and Tans, *bunch of wans*.

St. Enda's poncy poesy was proof
that righteous *Patrick Pearse was such a poof*.

      *

Because everyone has their story
I include mine here:
Learning to drive on the dusk-blue road
between my place and Ballycastle,
a figure stumbles before me
in the dark – a policeman, differential
from the night by nothing –
and asks me where I'm coming from
and where I'm headed to.
He's stopped us by a gate
that leads into the gaping black of a field
where just for a second I clock the flat form
of a camouflaged man, the moon glinting
off the glass-eye of his scope.

As I pull away I see the policeman
in the mirror, turning towards the field
and shaking his head, 'no luck',
before he disappears around the bend.

      *

When Thomas Ashe refused to eat
they held him down
and inserted a tube into his throat,
through which
they poured the jaundiced mulch
of his food. There was deep
guttural choking as he died. The Crown
maintained he suffocated in his sleep.

*

History was moving fast.
'...six times in the past...'
What times? Which times?
In the hills, around a cabbage patch?
Give us wars, give us blood,
not these feeble insurrections,
one night stands and volley blasts.

Give us what we want to see,
not the truth of history.

*

Civil War, *such a bore.*
Cromwell, *go to hell.*
Old King Billy? *What a dick!*

*

How we sat on the edge of our seats
as he told us of guns being run off the pier
at Howth. How we thought it would put out
their noses to have an essay defend De Valera,
how we never got any the nearer to knowing
the truth of Casement's trial, but later learnt
he was turning tricks in the Congo for a while.

How our stomachs would rumble in the period
leading to lunch, how we began to resemble
a clan or a movement or such – the historian buffs –
how we peered at the texts as the sexy peered at the toughs.
How we came to believe in one history just as he told it,
how we painted our faces and made our way into the market.

Generations

I find you often on the footpath by Lough Foyle,
your slow pace slower in the facing wind,
dragging behind you a broom of dulse,
and murmuring, softly, to the seabirds

about netting laws and rigging, the fluctuation
of the tides. I'll be on my way to catch
the ferryboat to Derry, you for a late fish supper
in Moville, and when I wave you will recognise me,

slowly, as in your mind you place just who I am,
how we are related, and then you'll beam and hustle
to my side, and look out to the teeming water,
and point at seabirds one by one:

'See there, that one's a cormorant, with its oil-slick neck,
and there is a lapwing, and there is the bar-tailed godwit.'
When I see you again I still won't know their names,
weaved in your light head as dulse knotted on sea beds.

Still Life with Five Nests

I sent a basket containing birds' nests to your address today. I have
some in my own studio too. They are nests of the thrush, the blackbird,
the golden oriole, the wren and the finch. I hope they will arrive safe
and sound.
　　　— Vincent Van Gogh, letter to Anthon van Rappard, 1885

When we examine a nest, we place ourselves at the origin of confidence
in the world.
　　　— Gaston Bachelard, *The Poetics of Space*

They are a pallet of pastels: mauve, pink,
a tiny speck of rouge. Fluttery, flighty,
my fingers pulled the knot out of the string,
unpicked the gum, let the brown paper fall,
revealing them, cuckolded in their square nest,
a selection of wild birds, a coterie of houses.
How must he have held them in his hands,
cupped them close and listened
for some noise of life beneath the shell,
a heartbeat nurtured by the warmth
of matted feathers. And the cleverness
of nests, the toil of days of labouring
at twigs and roots, this one a grassy cup,
and this a ball of leaves, its strength the folly
in its disrepair. This one would be high
in the forks of slender trees, lodged fast
to the bark in the late May winds. I can
only just surmise what is hidden in their
tight warmth, a narrative of craftsmanship
and brood, daily attachment. A song thrush
smashing snail shells for the flesh,
a blackbird darting full tilt from the cat.
Boys paid fifty cents to prise them
from the bushes and the trees, an artist
who would collect them, paint them,
summon up the birds careering round
the cornfields, hold them in his hands
against the black canvas: whole, flightless.

41

Fashion Show, Natural History Museum, February 2007

for Jens, Alastair, Sally, Rudi and the rest

Capture this: the bulbs, the flash, the people
leaning in on seated people, the music
tempered, steady, ready, and then the silent
apprehensive strain as there she is,
her many seldom selves, back arched, porcelain,
a band of crystals shimmering her thighs,
each step she takes so measured, unsurprised.
One imagines backstage being all a fight,
frenzied arguments, cracked heels, a ladder
in the tights, the rush to lift and pin,
the tightened hush. But now they've mastered
movement, made everything cohere to focus
eyes on fabric, shimmer-stick and blush.
She could almost take flight, turns incarnated
at the gangway's end, a Lewes bird of paradise
thrown flirtatious up into the lights,
startled from the darkness by the gasps.

The Seagull

for Milorad Krystanovich

We talked of seagulls, both children of the sea,
of coasts, and rocks and sand and stretching water.
Seagulls over Symphony Hall, fat bulbs of birds
pecking at the windows of the Tea Rooms.
You poured the tea. From Dalmatia you had brought
me a shell, plucked from the beach, a little amphora
cleansed by salt, years, rubbed free of sand by fingers.
'Why are the seagulls here?' you asked, tracing with pen
round the shell, and added, 'They are like me.'
What I bring you in return is basalt, and a large
smooth stone from the beach at Runkerry.
Milorad, my memories are black rocks beneath bare feet,
thighs sore from dunes, the smell of hardened seaweed
and the cold cold of a squall settling in, and the seagulls,
huge full flocks of them, soaring over the house towards the hills.

Fresh Water Cure

Hold back your head. I will place onto your eyes
the makings of whiskey: clear peat-bog water
from the River Bush, life-water, nutritious
with minnow and soft reeds and salmon scales,
to cleanse your intimate scabs, these diver's goggles
 – and malted barley, studs of hops and yeast,
pulped to a creamy paste, to rub
into your lids, creased and flaked as sun
mixed with salt water, the chapped earth.

All year I've been concocting remedies like this,
dunking all your illnesses in Irish waters: the Lagan
for deficiency of iron, the Liffey for your head,
the Lower Bann and Foyle to clear the lungs,
the shaken trickles from Lough Neagh to ease the blood.

We began by standing tall in shallow rivers,
learnt to walk against the water's pulsing charge.
Hand me your glass. Let me ladle up
the Shannon's lengthy waters for the both of us,
feel it rumble over rocks, smooth them to pebbles.

Green Men

Because of your broken toe, sharp-stubbed on the side
of the bed, and my flat-walker's charm of a foot,
we limp, on my twenty-fifth birthday, through
the snow and across the bridge to the wetlands
at Walthamstow.
                        Shovelers, widgeons, little grebes –
we count these birds amongst the new ones on our list,
add to them the stonechats on the Marsh, the green
woodpecker living, somehow, by the stench of Dagenham Brook.
The air is still, and all around the ponds cling sheets of ice.

I often wonder how we got like this,
fully-binoculared members of our private club:
just you and me whispering across the cold air,
lifting the wooden windows of the hide
to peer at what might not be there, and only
might exist if we're not spotted. We know
ducks don't mind, of course, nor geese nor coots,
but there was the stomach-sinking time I checked my watch
and missed the red-throated diver as it soared
with a rickety screech over our heads,
and I had to take your word for it.

I just had to take your word for it. My love,
the myth I always liked the most
was that of Featherboy, the Crow Indian
estranged and wandering in the desert,
who followed three birds – because he saw them
and felt their call – towards a clearing filled with buffalo,
then returned with the news to his starving tribe.

And as if it happened yesterday, or is happening right now,
I remember the morning we rose from the timidity and exhaustion
of the night and took the graveyard park
and read the names and noted gaps in years,
and shivered at the quietness of birds.

Like something nestled and defended and upheld:
when I guessed and guessed again the names of trees,
you gave me clues in bark-types and the shapes of leaves.

The Lake Effect

Graeme

Starkers again, listening to Elgar while the preening men around you gas about their latest conquests. Such pleasure in August – sparrows everywhere as the ferry puttered towards Hanlon Point, then the slow walk to the beach, the energized strip, the slap of lotion and the sheer inexhaustible excitement of the sun tingling your skin. Nothing lewd or insidious; private, nonetheless. You fought for this: petitions all along Church Street in '99. You fought for so much more, not hard to tell. But the lake affects you differently each year, and in winter it will freeze, and black ice will take the streets: such difference, such isolation.

Amar

3am. You're restless. You spent the best part of the day on the telephone to your brother, his first night in a cell in San Diego. Shoplifting handbags. Rather than sweat in sheets or try to read, you dress, drive slowly to the beach at Scarborough. The dim horizon and the grey sand. You can hear the maple flag in the breeze on Scarborough Bluffs. You love it here, the pull of water, the lake wide as the ocean. You're smoking more and more, and you light one now. Returning here, the first winter was hard. Though you knew it well you couldn't believe the black sky that comes over the city, the lake effect. You think of Trinidad, of the cigarettes glowing there in the fingers you know and don't know.

Graeme

When he was gone all that long year in England you thought at first coping would be fine; you'd coped with so much more. But autumn weakened into winter, the temperature hit 30 below. It was your third year in Toronto. From your balcony the Core was a cold inertia, nothing like the cold you'd known in the north; it was caustic, almost. You waited until the right hour of the day and called across the Atlantic; what was he doing? You remembered cricket and cream teas, an English Ale. Less bitter winters? He told you of lagers and curries, of hangovers, of every lecture ending in the pub. You had only known him fleetingly, three years of your life. Got up in your blankets, the windows bolted shut, you found comfort in stars in the snow-desert, huskies pulling you through the woods.

Amar

You wake again. Something has happened. Your Grandmother's bed is empty. The panic rises, but is gone at once. You see her on the balcony, leaning over the railing, watching the transvestites fight for their corners. Her first time in Toronto. She's seen nothing like it. You tell her of the hosers who come from out of town intent on beating them up, throwing their tits on the road, kicking their balls. She takes this in. You wonder how much she knows about you, how far you've come since Trinidad. You remember your move here, the way you'd avoid the Village, or rush across it; the way you thought you should be repulsed. Just five years ago. You split with the girl you'd been seeing and one night had a few beers, skirted past then walked back onto Church Street. Graeme was there. He showed you round. You took him down to the lake.

Pub Crawl

*Did the Warwickshire militia, who were chiefly artisans, teach the Irish
to drink beer, or did they learn from the Irish to drink whiskey?*
　　　　　　　　　— Maria Edgeworth, *Castle Rackrent*

1. Bushmills

Sometimes the river –
peaty blacks and browns –
looks laced with whiskey.
Uisce Beatha: the water of life.

When the salmon died
and floated pink on the water
(a major local scandal),
the rumour ran they'd all got drunk and drowned.

Each time I see the name
BUSHMILLS
on the top shelf
at my local cornershop

I remember those fish
staring up from their stupor,
smiling the way drunks do
and telling bawdy jokes.

'Two naked women
walk into a bar.
Which one's the alcoholic?

The one with the Black Bush.'

2. Foster's

'The Aussies call it Kangaroo Piss
and wouldn't touch it
with a bargepole.'
My old Australian uncle
drank glass after glass
of Irish whiskey,
diluted with tap water.

He said the water kept his wife at bay,
a liquid bridle.

3. Rum

Mythologies blend.

I think of my grandfather
tanked on pale poteen,
climbing Slemish
in an early morning mist

remembering his first journey
out from Hull,
the swaying, sloshing hull
of the Merchant Navy

learning to drink
strong Caribbean rum
and raising a toast in the mess
to seamen lost and Murphy One-Ear.

4. Guinness

I've heard that a true
pint of Guinness
needs to have its head
sliced off with a knife,

that the barman
will wait till it's settled
then skim round the rim
like a trained butcher.
In Leamington Spa,
in an Irish pub
with a tuneless bodhran,
my pint was all black,

the head slopped off
when the barman
spilt it, botching
away the beauty.

5. Wine

'Turning water into wine
is no mean feat.'

When we start talking
about religion

I think we've had enough.

The Moose

New England, 1999

My mum and I were dozing as he hit the brakes
somewhere on the roads between Squam Lake
and Lake Winnipesaukee (dozing in the heat
as dozers do when the journey's long, streets
of one-road towns melted black, roadsides burnt
brown, weeds bursting from grey flints,
and inside the car the sweat of hard gums
and the same-same bass, pedal, drums
of local indy music, and the air con
up to its old tricks: *If the window's down
it doesn't work pete's sakes!*) – he pushed
the brakes, the Corolla stopped, and the land hushed
around us, no wind in heat. Softly, my dad said
'moose' like the first thing he'd uttered
for days, and there, sure enough, was the moose,
drolly crossing the highway, reclusive,
hornless, heavy with child. We were the one
car in fifty miles. The moose looked once
then slouched into the trees.
                              What a summer
that was, NYC, Connecticut, New Hampshire,
just the three of us alone in the hired car,
skirting through forests, stopping at pool bars,
engulfing cafes, restrooms, shopping malls,
then the lakes and wide beaches, and motels
like a dream come true, all slatted white
and balconies on the water, birds in flight
and silent in the blueness, their taut accord.

Allowed to stay up late and play cards,
to choose where we went, have a few sips of wine,
and I properly got into boys for the first time,
watched them diving off the raft, young
bodies play-fighting, those swelling lungs.
I learnt to snorkel, to listen to my head
below the water, and we were so darn well fed

on platters, burgers, fries, that even I, skinny as skate,
managed to garner a stone in weight.

History is the patterns we make:
snatches of smiles, long-forgotten tastes, half-baked
murmurs at the back of the mind
that urge and tease, niggle into being. Determined,
we'd set out to rescue my sister from a Baptists'
soaking and found her insistent,
unwearied, a different person. Did I just
make that last bit up? I who then fussed
for accuracy. Forgive me, mother, father.
I don't know. There's only what I've gathered,
and it's all been pressed, squeezed, sluiced.
But I'll never forget that moose.

The Summer-house

I have not read them, but they are here in a box
on the table, letters from my mother to my father,
one letter a week for three years, apart from
holidays when they courted at Belfast Castle,
or the cinema on the Antrim Road, or, later,
when he went to the mainland to join her for
a summer picking strawberries in Evesham, when
they did not talk of letters or what was said in them –
the ice wind hitting Redcar, and the English girls
who always went for trouble, or news of bombs,
how he should quit the ciggies – but instead gave up
the tenderness of words for quiet solid plans
of hearth and home, of languorous days in the summer-house,
watching sea swells and fields being ploughed,
with a cup of tea and the papers, a whole basket of shells.

At Last

there is some colour in the house.
Quite amazing, how these four daffodils
have made this room so bright, made the blank walls
painted, the light come back into the space.

It's all so simple. Pick them from the sides
of busy roads, their petals grey with fumes.
Then put them in a jam-jar. Now you've made
an ornament, a pet, a fire, a home,

now an installation, a mausoleum.
I never thought I'd love such sentiment,
and did not think I'd dare to talk of pain.
I didn't want to take the easy slant

on things. Did not intend. But here we are,
a room, one window, four yellow flowers.

The Granite State

New Hampshire, 1845. The Amoonoosuc River
tumbles white and grey below Mount Washington,
where, like factory-carts in the black pits
of the north, they spill towards the summit.

Eight horses, heavy laden with buckets, satchels,
notebooks and knives, navigating through boulders
on the well-worn path, a stodgy mule taking
the rear, hooves cracking on dark flints.

Lyell, the geologist, a butterfly-net pendulating
from his saddle like a metronome as they pitch
up-hill, hoiks a piece of rock from the tundra
and scrapes the lichen delicately onto a glass.

He loves these moments when he gets into the field,
caresses the elements, lets his mind feed. He notes
how the cloud-shadows unveil the banded colours
of the trees, and the lakes shining like silver.

Yesterday, with the kind guidance of locals,
he stood in the clearing at Crawford's Notch,
where the land slipped one afternoon and crushed
the Willey family without a moment's notice –

all nine out with the crops, or painting
the white fences, thoughts on the evening meal,
they turned to see the mountain fall and could not run.
They left life in the sudden shift, the glacial past.

Arctic plants and hemlock. Balsam fir, white pine
and spruce. He breathes wide mountain air.
Still young, he thinks, eyeing the valley,
still young enough to change the world again.

He thinks mountains and landscape and lineage.
He thinks granite. He is thinking of the Highlands
he walked in his youth, of the island of Arran.
He sees in the granite the kindred thing.

Fair Head

She made her bedroom so it didn't face
the other houses of the clachan, but instead
looked only at the place where sky was a lung-tug
of gravity on the edge of the cliff,
a drop to boulders, granite-spikes, the channel of sea.
This was her retirement. No more the large house
she couldn't heat, no more the stairs,
only the two rooms, the scuttle, the knick-knacks,
the breath of the wind in the night and the day.
She'd go as she came, in a bed a foot from the soil,
in a cottage without running water, with the yelp
of the dogs in the field, the odd hovering falcon,
and every so often when the day was clear
the cliff-face and mountains of Scotland.

An Invitation

from north Antrim
to my lover

after Thom Gunn

If, one day, you can visit me at home,
I'll put you in the large well-lighted room
at my home's front, where you will wake to sounds
of cattle moving to the barn, and winds
that circle, soothe and nurture the old house
(my too familiar winds) as a sharp douse
of winter magic shaking in the eaves.
From scalded pot, a sprinkle of fresh leaves,
I'll bring you a strong cup of Irish tea,
and through the window we will watch the sea
get its mileage on the jagged basalt rocks,
and throw up foam, and toss the raft of ducks,
and sink its tapered fingers in the sand.
You will point at birds; I will take your hand.

Later we will head out to the fields
in wellies and thick coats, where crispness bleeds
an auburn line on tree fenced boundaries,
a haze that makes the whole land seem to wheeze.
Then I'll show you the castle at Carnkirk,
and in the fields we'll watch the tractors work
the furrows from the ground, and we might chat
to men whose gruntled accents you won't get,
their 'thons' and 'sheughs' totally beyond you.
  Dunseverick, Bushmills, Lisnagunogue –
I'll take you to the places that I know
as places from a life which somehow slowed
with history. I don't think that we'll linger,
for of course we'll want a pub, a finger
of whiskey, a black pint, a cosy spot
somewhere in the nook, the snug, to eat hot
broth and watch the people come and laugh and talk
of pheasant shoots, depleting fishing stocks.

And then the walk home in the blackest dark,
to let our pathway be the timid marks
of beasts who followed wind-chill, moonlight, clocks
built in by nature. The back door unlocked
we'll trudge through, kick off the mud. Inside they'll
have kindled up a fire, and we will fill
the kettle for more tea. We'll spend the night
there, wind shuddering the panes, curled up tight
with books, working letters into puzzles
for new words: each consonant, each vowel.

Reprieve

For the sake of recovery: the county of chalk.
Wind in one furious push at West Kennett
Long Barrow, the river green below and flooded.
Inside, stone laid heavily on stone and recent
offerings: flowers, feathers, marbles, a dead mouse.

We return to light. The horizontal rain ochres
the hay-bales, and sarsens loom like strangers
on the hillside. A smell of hash kicks the air
and disappears. They're tying ribbons to the trees.
The valley is still. That nothing changed

in a thousand years, heads and parts of bodies
placed here in the darkness, a ritual never
written down or carved in rock, while fields
stayed green and water ran its course, is alien to us.
We alter daily, and find our histories malleable.